Adventures in Cartooning

Create a World

James Sturm, Andrew Arnold, and Alexis Frederick-Frost

:01
First Second
New York

b

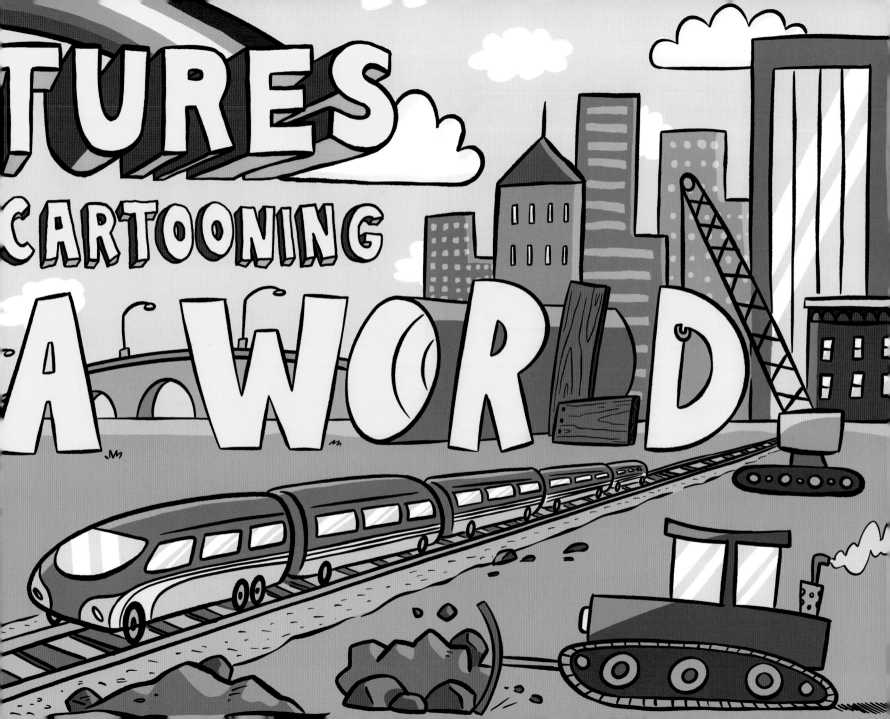

19

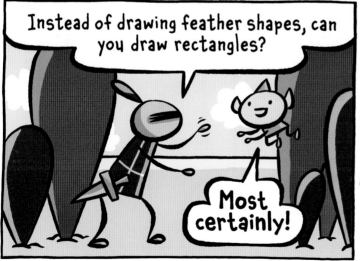

25

Stupid Elf!

STUPID EDWARD!

He said he'd help, too, and all he did was draw candy!

ONE YEAR, TWO MONTHS, AND SIX DAYS LATER...

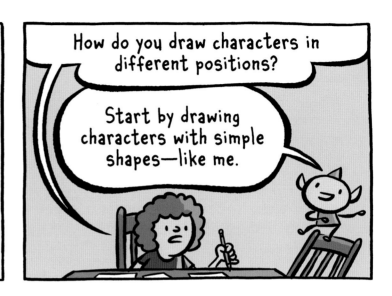

How do you draw characters in different positions?

Start by drawing characters with simple shapes—like me.

Is it okay to copy other comics when I draw?

YES! It's a great way to learn!

Do I know you?

Do I **always** need panel borders or word balloons?

No, you don't!

I never, ever, ever, ever, ever, ever, **EVER**, have enough room in my **WORD BALLOONS** for my lettering. It's so <u>frustrating.</u>

Hmm...

If you letter **first**, then draw the word balloon, you'll **always** have enough room!

If you letter **first**, then draw the word balloon, you'll **always** have enough room!

See?

I DID IT! I'm all caught up...

Oops, not yet! One more person still needs me!

POOF

I started thinking about what you showed me.

Using simple shapes, I drew my desert island bigger and made it taller, like adding layers to a cake.

I then drew all the different trees and plants I could think of...

I also needed a place to live on the island—and a place for all the secret agents who worked for me—so I drew as many different places as I could think of.

Log cabins

Houses

Tents

Amphitheaters

Firehouses

Doghouses

Chicken coops

Geothermal pools

Huts

Lighthouses

Towers

Igloos

Windmills and wind turbines

Solar panels

(Plus all kinds of ways to power the island!)

Not all my ideas made sense (an igloo on a tropical island?!), but some of them did! I was really proud of how **AMAZING** my secret headquarters was looking. I was now ready for a secret mission!

My plan was to find secret agents in a big city. Cities are really complicated to draw, but I felt I was ready to try after drawing my island. I started jotting down all the things that make a city a city...

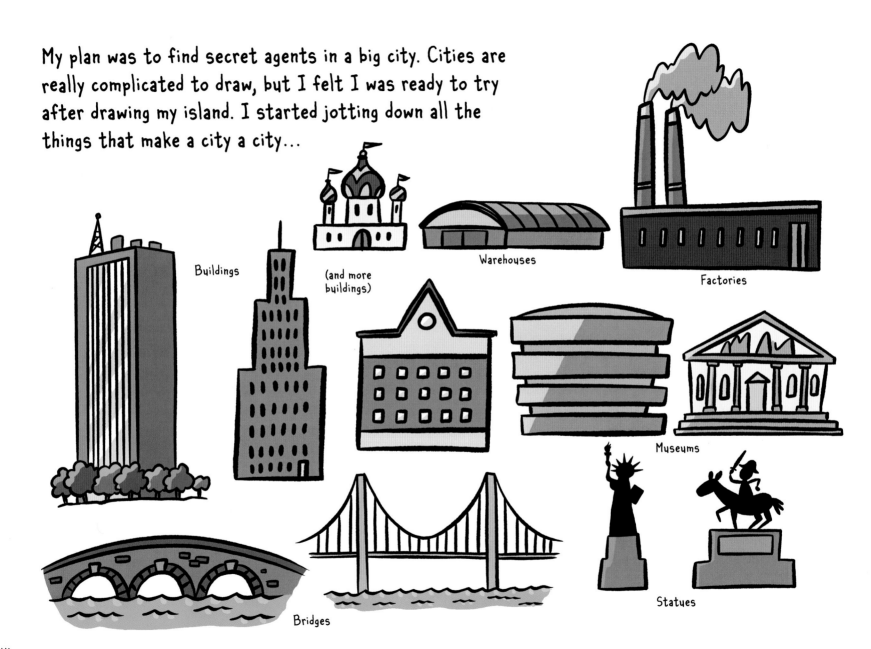

Buildings

(and more buildings)

Warehouses

Factories

Museums

Bridges

Statues

The list kept going and going. When you think about it, there's a lot of stuff that goes into making a city a city... I had to look at pictures to remind myself of everything!

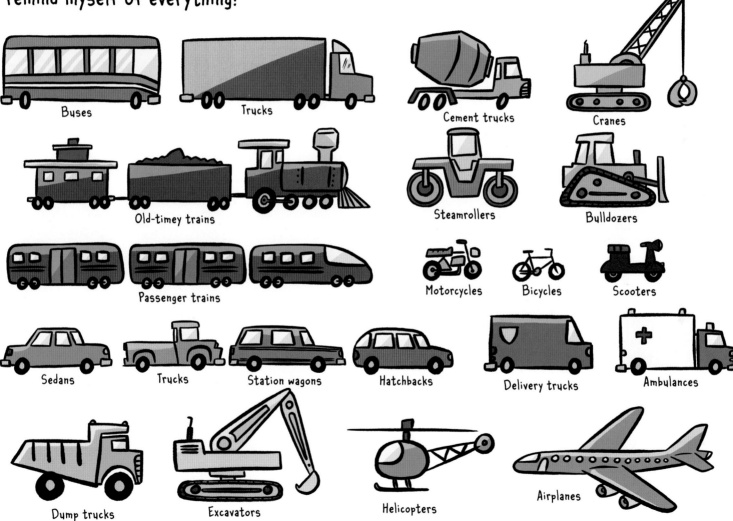

Buses

Trucks

Cement trucks

Cranes

Old-timey trains

Steamrollers

Bulldozers

Passenger trains

Motorcycles

Bicycles

Scooters

Sedans

Trucks

Station wagons

Hatchbacks

Delivery trucks

Ambulances

Dump trucks

Excavators

Helicopters

Airplanes

It took me A LOT of tries, but I finally put everything together. I imagined all the people who live in a city!

THIS was where my story would take place!

51

Next, I headed to the stadium.

Maybe there will be some double agents at this doubleheader.

I went to the theater, but it was hard to tell who was in disguise and who was in costume.

I wasn't sure of anything anymore. Who was who? Where to go?

It's funny, but somewhere along the way, my world...

...started to feel **real**.

All the little details.

It was full of energy. Of **life**...

But I
wanted more.

Something was wrong, but I wasn't sure what.

Was I sleepy?

Did I need a nap?

Was I hungry? Thirsty?

No. Something was missing from this world. Something important.

So I went back...

...and underwater empires.

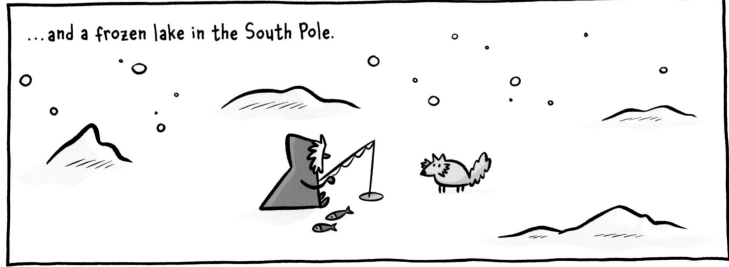

I drew cities that floated in the sky...

...and other planets in the far reaches of outer space.

Hundreds and hundreds of worlds...

...each one unique and distinct.

I drew so much...

...that my hand started to hurt. But that wasn't the only part of me in pain.

My heart hurt, too.

That's when I finally realized what each of these worlds lacked...

70

73

75

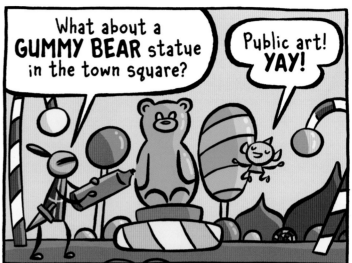

I can use the **COTTON CANDY** stick from earlier as a flagpole...

...and a stick of **BUBBLE GUM** as a flag!

Above it all...a **LEMON DROP** sun!

DRAW WITH

Brush

Feather

Colored pencils

Crayons

Stick

Q-tip

Pen and nib

Broken crayons

Thick and thin markers

Colored markers

You can dip things into ink and draw with them!

Mechanical pencil

Pencil

Stubby pencil with no eraser

It's fun to try them all!

DRAW ON

CRAFT PAPER
on a roll!

COPY PAPER
Use new sheets
or draw on the
back of used ones!

LINED PAPER
is fine paper!
Rip it out or
leave it in!

BRISTOL OR POSTER BOARD
Sturdier than paper, so it's better for
watercolors. Plus you can erase on it more!

INDEX CARDS
Every card is its
own panel!

STICKY NOTES
Same deal as index
cards!

CARDBOARD
Why not?!

Draw on any
paper except
toilet paper!

It's good to have lots of paper on hand...

...because making comics can get messy!

You can always replace and combine parts of drawings to make new ones.

CUT and

PASTE or GLUE or

GLUE STICK or RUBBER CEMENT!
You can use TAPE, too!

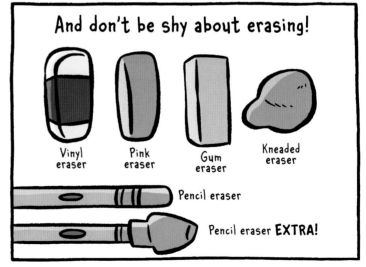

And don't be shy about erasing!

Vinyl eraser

Pink eraser

Gum eraser

Kneaded eraser

Pencil eraser

Pencil eraser EXTRA!

THE END!

Also available!

The book that
started it all!

Characters
abound!

:01

First Second

Published by First Second
First Second is an imprint of Roaring Brook Press,
a division of Holtzbrinck Publishing Holdings Limited Partnership
120 Broadway, New York, NY 10271
firstsecondbooks.com

Library of Congress Control Number: 2022920203

Our books may be purchased in bulk for promotional, educational, or business use.
Please contact your local bookseller or the Macmillan Corporate and Premium Sales Department at
(800) 221-7945 ext. 5442 or by email at MacmillanSpecialMarkets@macmillan.com.

First edition, 2023
Edited by Mark Siegel and Tess Banta
Cover design by Alexis Frederick-Frost, Andrew Arnold, James Sturm, Yan L. Moy, and Molly Johanson
Interior book design by Andrew Arnold, Alexis Frederick-Frost, and Molly Johanson
Additional coloring assistance by Mercedes Campos López
Production editing by Helen Seachrist and Sarah Gompper

This book was created by passing little doodles back and forth between Alexis, Andrew, and James.
Then a lot of those doodles got redrawn a few times and then colored on a computer.
Lettered digitally with a font based on Andrew Arnold's handwriting. He has the nicest handwriting of all the authors.

This series began at the Center for Cartoon Studies in White River Junction, Vermont. Yes, a college for cartoonists: cartoonstudies.org

Printed in China by RR Donnelley Asia Printing Solutions Ltd., Dongguan City, Guangdong Province

ISBN 978-1-250-83941-1
10 9 8 7 6 5 4 3 2 1

Don't miss your next favorite book from First Second!
For the latest updates go to firstsecondnewsletter.com and sign up for our enewsletter.

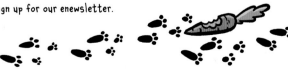